**PEOPLE
WHO MADE
A DIFFERENCE**

DESMOND TUTU

Other titles in the
PEOPLE WHO MADE A DIFFERENCE
series include

Louis Braille
Marie Curie
Father Damien
Mahatma Gandhi
Bob Geldof
Martin Luther King, Jr.
Ralph Nader
Florence Nightingale
Albert Schweitzer
Mother Teresa
Sojourner Truth

North American edition first published in 1991 by
Gareth Stevens Children's Books
1555 North RiverCenter Drive, Suite 201
Milwaukee, Wisconsin 53212, USA

This edition is abridged from *Desmond Tutu: The courageous and eloquent archbishop struggling against apartheid in South Africa*, copyright © 1989 by Exley Publications Ltd. and written by David Winner. Additional end matter copyright © 1991 by Gareth Stevens, Inc.

For a free color catalog describing Gareth Stevens' list of high-quality children's books, call

1-800-341-3569 (USA) or
1-800-461-9120 (Canada)

Library of Congress Cataloging-in-Publication Data

Lantier, Patricia, 1952-
    Desmond Tutu.
        p. cm. — (People who made a difference)
    "Patricia Lantier's adaptation of the book by David Winner."
    Includes index.
    Summary: Examines the life of the South African bishop and civil rights worker who has worked extensively to improve conditions for his fellow citizens.
    ISBN 0-8368-0459-7
    1. Tutu, Desmond. 2. South Africa—Race relations. 3. Church of the Province of South Africa—Bishops—Biography. 4. Anglican Communion—South Africa—Bishops—Biography. [1. Tutu, Desmond. 2. Civil rights workers. 3. Clergy. 4. Blacks—Biography. 5. South Africa—Race relations.] I. Winner, David, 1956- Desmond Tutu. II. Title. III. Series.
BX5700.6.Z8T8746   1990   283'.092—dc20
[B]   [92]   90-10044

PICTURE CREDITS

Associated Press — 4; Omar Badsha — 46; BBC Hulton Picture Library: Mal Langsdon — 45 (top left); Camera Press: Jacob Sutton — 30; Durand — 11, 58 (top); Greg English — 36, 40, 49; Fair Lady — 54 (both); Gunston — 51 (above); Chips Hire — 45 (below right); International Defence and Aid Fund for Southern Africa — 8, 9 (both), 10, 12, 15 (both), 17, 22, 23, 26, 28, 35, 36 (top), 47 (below); J. Kuus — 58 (below); Link: Jillian Edelstein — 42, 47 (top); Orde Eliason — 29, 33, 38, 42 (top right and bottom left), 59 (top); Peter Magubane — 34; Photo Source: C. Friend — 7; Popperfoto — 16, 21; Tom Redman — cover; Reflex: Philip Littleton — 59 (below); Reuters: Wendy Schwegmann — 53; Rex Features — 37; Rogan Coles — 44; Frank Spooner: J. Chiasson — 51 (below); Desmond Tutu — 19, 31; U.S.P.G.: Bryan Heseltine — 6.

Maps drawn by Geoffrey Pleasance.

Series conceived and edited by Helen Exley
Series editor, U.S.: Amy Bauman
Editor, U.S.: Tom Barnett
Editorial assistants, U.S.: Scott Enk, Diane Laska, John D. Rateliff
Cover design: Kate Kriege

Printed in the United States of America

1 2 3 4 5 6 7 8 9 95 94 93 92 91

Religious leader devoted to freedom

DESMOND TUTU

Patricia Lantier

David Winner

Gareth Stevens Children's Books
MILWAUKEE

973394

Protest in Cape Town

Black South African people fighting for freedom received bad news on February 4, 1988. The government was making it illegal for any group to oppose it. The news shocked everyone who was struggling for freedom in South Africa.

Now the United Democratic Front, a group of people of all races, had been silenced by the government. Sixteen other freedom groups were broken up, too. Police arrested all the leaders. South Africa's white leaders would not let anyone speak out against them.

The government had been all white for many years. The black people had no freedom and no way to make changes in the government. White rule was cruel and unfair. This type of system is called apartheid. The word means "apart-hood."

Most antiapartheid leaders were now in jail. The only groups left to fight the government were the churches.

Archbishop Desmond Tutu, a respected black church leader, called a special meeting of religious leaders in South Africa. They met at his cathedral in Cape

"[We are not] the usual bunch of rabble-rousers."
Desmond Tutu, at a news conference of clergymen defending the church's right to protest apartheid

Opposite: Archbishop Desmond Tutu (middle) marches toward the police lines in Cape Town to protest the government's banning of opposition groups. With him are the other religious leaders, now the only remaining voice of opposition to apartheid. On the left is Allan Boesak; on the right is Archbishop Stephen Naidoo. All were arrested for this protest.

Many of South Africa's 21 million blacks are forced by the government to live in crowded conditions without electricity, running water, or sewers. The racist system of apartheid makes poverty among blacks a sure thing. In the rich, beautiful land of South Africa, blacks have no political or economic say in their own futures.

Town to protest on February 29, 1988. Leaders from many Christian churches went to the cathedral. They prayed together, and then they linked arms and marched from the church toward the government offices a short distance away.

The marchers wanted to give a letter to the prime minister. A line of armed riot police blocked their path. One officer told the group to go home.

The marchers refused and knelt on the ground. The police did not know what to do with the marchers. Finally, policemen arrested Archbishop Tutu and others.

Tutu was a well known church leader. The police were afraid to keep these important religious leaders in prison too long. But the South African government thought this peaceful protest was just a way of causing trouble.

White rulers wanted to take away what few rights the blacks had. They passed many laws against the black people. Blacks had lived in Africa for thousands of years before white people arrived. But now they had no freedom at all in their own country.

Many whites had servants and houses with swimming pools. Most blacks lived in poor conditions with no electricity, water, or toilets.

Apartheid's unfair laws forced black fathers to leave their areas to find work. Thousands of blacks had to get up at three o'clock in the morning and travel long distances to work each day. Blacks were not allowed to live in the cities unless they worked as servants.

There are five times as many black people as white in South Africa. But the blacks were not allowed to vote. They had no voice in their government.

Black families who had lived in their homes for many years had to move. White officials could order them to live in terrible places hundreds of miles away.

Anyone who refused could be beaten and put in prison. The government even

On the other side of the racial divide, many of South Africa's four-and-a-half-million whites live in surroundings like those shown here in Stellenbosch. White homes have running water, electricity, and trash collection.

White settlers began treating blacks badly hundreds of years ago. This picture depicting seventeenth-century South Africa shows black workers being supervised by white settlers in the early days of the Cape Colony.

tried to stop people from protesting peacefully. Black South Africans did not know what to do.

The first whites

Unfair treatment of one race by another is called racial discrimination. In South Africa, discrimination by white people against black people has been going on for about 350 years.

The first Europeans to live in South Africa were Dutch. They settled at the Cape of Good Hope, the very tip of Africa, in 1652. The Dutch East India Company sent ships there to get fresh food, water, and fuel. Dutch traders and sailors liked the warm climate and beautiful land.

Many ancient tribes lived in South Africa at the time the Dutch settled there. The San and Khoikhoi tribes were two prominent tribes in the area where the settlers first set up their towns. They were gentle, trusting people. At first, the white settlers got along well with the local people. But this did not last long. The whites began to steal food from the natives. The Khoikhoi fought back, but the whites had guns. Bows, arrows, and spears were not much help. Many thousands of Africans died in battle.

Boatloads of Europeans arrived from Germany, France, and the Netherlands. These people conquered the blacks and settled on their land. The Cape became a colony of European nations. Most of the new people were farmers known as Boers, a name that comes from a Dutch word

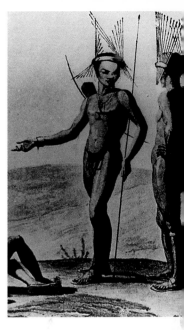

Above: Africans suffered at the hands of early settlers. Below: Boers fight the Xhosa in the Wars of Dispossession.

During the Great Trek, Boer settlers, called Voortrekkers, fought attacking Zulu in the Battle of Vegkop. The Zulu armies fought bravely, but their spears and shields were no match for the Boers' rifles. The Boers formed their own country by taking over all land in the center of South Africa.

meaning "farmer." The Boers even had their own language — Afrikaans.

The Cape became a terrible place for native Africans. The Boers treated them like slaves. They also brought thousands of black people from other parts of Africa to work in the colony and help the white settlers get rich. Those who tried to run away were punished or killed.

The British take over

Britain took over the country in 1814. They tried to rule over both the Boers and the Africans.

The British were just as cruel as the Dutch. They, too, did not think that black people should have equal rights. But

they did stop the slave trade. They also told the Boers that they had to set all of their slaves free.

The Boers disliked the British. They did not want to give up their control of the black people. They wanted to keep their slaves and continue using them for all of the hard work that needed to be done. They began to protest against the British government that was now ruling the land.

The "Great Trek"

The British refused to change their antislavery laws. Thousands of Boers decided to move away from the Cape. They decided to set up their own country in what is now the northeastern section of South Africa. This "Great Trek" took place between 1835 and 1840.

Today, Afrikaners (descendants of the original Dutch settlers) still remember the Great Trek. They are proud of their ancestors and celebrate their bravery every year. The Boers who made the long journey are called "Voortrekkers."

The Voortrekkers thought they were moving to an empty land. But they were really invading other African territories. They fought native armies who tried to defend their land.

The Zulu were the most powerful tribe. But even the mighty Zulu spears could not stop Boer rifles and cannons. The

"History, like beauty, depends largely on the beholder so when you read that, for example, David Livingstone discovered the Victoria Falls, you might be forgiven for thinking that there was nobody around the Falls until Livingstone arrived on the scene."

Desmond Tutu, on the twentieth anniversary of the South African Republic

Afrikaners are proud of the Great Trek, which they celebrate each year. They dress in Voortrekker clothes to celebrate their defeat of the Zulu in 1838.

Diamond mines at Kimberley in the 1870s. The discovery of diamonds and gold brought great wealth to whites but only suffering to the blacks who worked in the mines. Note how the artist has depicted the cruelty of the boss at left.

Boers formed two new countries: the Orange Free State and Transvaal. The blacks who had lived on their own land before now became slaves of the Boers, who were no longer under the control of the British Empire.

Gold and diamonds

When diamonds were discovered in Kimberley, South Africa, in the 1860s, the British decided to claim the mine for

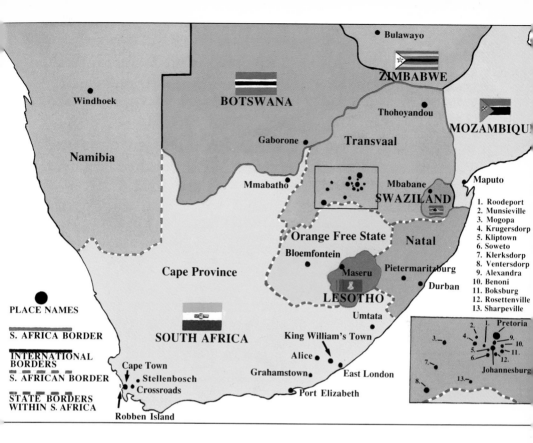

Place Names

S. AFRICA BORDER

INTERNATIONAL BORDERS

S. AFRICAN BORDER

STATE BORDERS WITHIN S. AFRICA

1. Roodeport
2. Munsieville
3. Mogopa
4. Krugersdorp
5. Kliptown
6. Soweto
7. Klerksdorp
8. Ventersdorp
9. Alexandra
10. Benoni
11. Boksburg
12. Rosettenville
13. Sharpeville

themselves. They fought and took control over most of the remaining tribes. Thousands of blacks were then forced to work in the mines. The British treated these men very badly. Even though the British had claimed to have gotten rid of slavery, the workers were treated just as badly as if they had been slaves.

Large gold fields were soon found in Transvaal. Together they stretched out to three hundred square miles (780 sq km). This was the largest amount of gold that had ever been discovered in one

South Africa and the surrounding countries, showing many of the important places in Desmond Tutu's life. In 1987, Tutu would become Anglican archbishop of South Africa, as well as of Lesotho, Namibia, Swaziland, and Mozambique.

13

place. The mines were seen as a great opportunity for wealth and power.

British colonists wanted the gold. They hoped to get rich in these huge fields. This greatly angered the Afrikaners. Both the Afrikaners and the British wanted control of the mines. This led to the Boer War in 1899. In this war, the Afrikaners took on the British Empire.

The Boer War lasted for three years. The Boers lost many people. More than twenty thousand of their women and children died in British prison camps. The British finally won the war in 1902.

Both sides had forced many thousands of blacks to fight. Many of these blacks lost their lives. But this fact is hardly ever written in history books.

"The South African government has signed its own death warrant. No government can take on the living God and survive."
Rev. Allan Boesak, president, World Alliance of Reformed Churches

New problems

Under the British, South Africa was finally united as the Union of South Africa.

The Afrikaners and the British made peace. The British even allowed the Afrikaners to have a voice in their government. This made life even worse for South Africa's black people. The whites called them *kaffirs* to insult them.

The blacks had been forced to live apart from the whites for many years. Now, whites took most of the country for themselves. Blacks could not vote. They could live only in certain areas. They also had to pay unfair taxes.

Above: A street scene in a typical black township.

Left: A family with no running water must make do with a tin bath outside.

This is the world into which Desmond Tutu was born. His bedroom was also the family dining and living room. He remarks that when he was young, he was a "township urchin" who went to school barefoot.

15

Young Desmond

Desmond Mpilo Tutu was born on October 7, 1931. He lived in Klerksdorp, a poor black area near Johannesburg, South Africa. Desmond Tutu's family was like many other black South African families. They did not have much money. Their home had no water, electricity, or indoor toilets.

The Tutus obeyed the same unfair laws as other black people. Desmond's father, Zachariah, was a respected schoolteacher. But he still had to carry a special passbook at all times. White police often stopped him in the street to look at his passbook. This upset young Desmond. It seemed very unfair to him.

The Tutu family was happy and loving. Desmond's mother, Aletha, worked as a servant for a white family. Desmond also had three sisters.

Desmond did not have many toys. But he and his friends still had fun. They played soccer with old tennis balls. They made model cars out of scraps of metal. Desmond sometimes sold oranges to make a little money. He was also a caddy at a golf club which allowed only white people to play.

Desmond did well in school. He was smart and worked very hard. But he could also be naughty. He and a friend rode a train to high school every day. They played cards with other passengers

Father Trevor Huddleston (shown below in 1957) campaigns against apartheid. He has inspired Tutu and has been his lifelong friend. Father Trevor became an archbishop and a leader of the antiapartheid movement in Britain.

and became experts at cheating. This was one way to get extra money.

Desmond always felt proud to hear stories about successful black people in other countries. He loved the music of famous black Americans like Louis Armstrong. He admired black athletes like Olympic gold medalist Jesse Owens.

As a child, Desmond realized that not all white people were cruel. He saw a tall white priest while walking with his mother one day. The priest smiled at Aletha Tutu and raised his hat in greeting. Desmond was surprised that a white person had been polite to them.

Desmond caught tuberculosis when he was fourteen years old. He was very ill and almost died. He had to stay in a hospital for almost two years. While there, Desmond made an important new friend. It was Father Trevor Huddleston, the friendly priest he had met years earlier while walking with his mother. Every day, Father Huddleston came to visit him. The priest talked with Desmond and brought him lots of books to read.

The apartheid election

South Africa held an election in 1948. Only whites could vote, and they chose the National party to lead the country. This election marked the beginning of the country's apartheid system. Now there would be even more antiblack laws.

"I wrote to the [prime minister] about . . . this policy of Black uprooting. . . . basically he was saying the removals are legal. Here in South Africa we tend to think that legal and morally right mean the same thing."
Desmond Tutu, in his book Hope and Suffering

In the 1950s, children demonstrated against the hated Group Areas Act. The law forces blacks, whites, and so-called Coloureds to live in separate parts of the country.

NON EUROPEANS NOT ADMITTED
RIGHT OF ADMISSION RESERVED
NO DOGS ALLOWED
DO NOT DAMAGE TREES/PLANTS

MEREDALE PLEASURE RESORT and (PTY LTD) CARAVAN PARK

Apartheid is a racist system. As apartheid became law in the years after 1948, signs banning blacks from "whites only" beaches, park benches, buses, and other public places appeared throughout the country. This is a "whites only" vacation resort at Meredale.

Life for black South Africans got worse right away. Terrible new laws passed quickly under the new government. Racial discrimination against blacks was now part of the law of South Africa.

The Prohibition of Mixed Marriages Act made marriages between whites and nonwhites illegal.

The Population Registration Act classified every person in the country by skin color. The four major groups were white, "Coloured" (people of mixed races), Asian, and "Native" (the word whites at that time used for blacks). These laws were set up to make it easier for the whites to control the other groups, which had many more people in them.

Laws for race grouping became even more confusing. In 1950, the four major classes each had several divisions of their own. "Coloureds" had seven groups; "Natives" had eight groups. Only the whites stayed as one group, even though their ancestors really came from many different countries.

The word *race* once meant "a group that shares a common ancestor." In the 1900s, biologists decided that human beings could be split into different groups, or races. But people are very much the same, no matter what their skin color. Race is really just skin-deep. All people belong to one race — the human race.

The South African government set up a special board to help decide which groups

"[Dr. Hendrik Verwoerd] said that since we could feed only some [black children] and not all, we must not feed even those we could. . . . Because you can't cure all TB patients don't cure those you can — would that be acceptable?"
Desmond Tutu,
in Hope and Suffering

Desmond and Leah Tutu on their wedding day, July 2, 1955. Leah was a powerful person in her own right. She would bring a sense of peace and happiness to Desmond in the years ahead.

19

some people belonged to. During the 1950s, this board held thousands of trials. Black families often were forced to split apart because the board said they belonged to different color groupings.

The government also passed laws stating that each race had to live in a different place. Whites did not want black people near them. Blacks had to live in "dumping grounds" outside the major cities. They had different schools, buses, and public toilets.

Desmond graduated from high school with honors in 1950. He was one of the few blacks able to attend a university. At first, he wanted to become a doctor. But his family did not have enough money to pay for medical school. So Desmond decided to become a teacher.

Desmond first met Leah Nomalizo Shenxane during this time. She also was a teacher. He fell in love with Leah and asked her to marry him in 1955. Their first child was a boy, whom they named Trevor, after Father Trevor Huddleston.

Tutu became a teacher at Munsieville High School in Krugersdorp. He often had as many as sixty students in one class. Desmond really liked teaching. But he would not be able to enjoy his new profession for very long.

The Bantu Education Act of 1955 was the most unjust law of all. Dr. Hendrik Verwoerd, apartheid leader of South

Until the 1970s, blacks often had to build their own schools. On the wall behind this student, who lives in the Eastern Transvaal, you can see the patterns children's fingers have made in the mud as they worked. Many students are too poor to buy schoolbooks.

Africa, created this law. He did not want blacks to be educated. Teachers could no longer teach anything useful or important to black children.

Dr. Verwoerd did not want black children to have good educations. He said blacks were meant to be servants for whites. They did not need to learn the same subjects that white children learned. This new law shocked black South Africa. Now the children would not receive a good education. Desmond Tutu was very angry about this racist policy. He did not want to be a teacher under this system.

Tutu turned to his faith for help. His family had always been religious, and Desmond was a strong Christian. He decided to join a theological college and become a priest. As Tutu later said: "I was grabbed by God by the scruff of the neck in order to spread His word, whether it is convenient or not."

Peaceful protest

Good people of all races protested the apartheid laws. They needed courage to fight this cruel and inhuman system.

The African National Congress (ANC) and the South African Indian Council (SAIC) were two groups that united to protest against apartheid. Brave men like Albert John Luthuli, Oliver Tambo, and Nelson Mandela led their people. The African National Congress always

Vernon Barrange, a lawyer defending antiapartheid leaders at the Treason Trial, is carried after their victory in 1961. All the defendants were found "not guilty." This four-year trial brought the problems in South Africa to the attention of the world. The South African government had been publicly humiliated.

The Sharpeville Massacre shocked the world. On March 21, 1960, sixty-nine men and women were killed by police during a demonstration against the hated Pass Laws. In South Africa, the police have often used violence to discourage nonviolent protest.

"Don't delay our freedom, which is your freedom as well, for freedom is indivisible."
Desmond Tutu,
in Hope and Suffering

protested peacefully. The members believed in nonviolence. The great Indian leader Mahatma Gandhi had developed and used this method against the British in India. Dr. Martin Luther King, Jr., used this method in the United States. Later, Desmond Tutu would use it, too.

The Defiance Campaign, as they called it, fought the apartheid laws by trying to shame the government into changing the laws. Protesters filled the prisons. They hoped to show that apartheid was like putting an entire people in jail.

Thousands of volunteers joined this protest. Black people at this time could not even walk in white cities at night. But the protesters were peaceful. They told police in advance which laws they would break. They demanded to be arrested and put in prison. They also tried to get the attention of journalists.

Various groups decided to band together. Opponents of apartheid united to form the National Action Council of the Congress of the People. In 1955 this group wrote a "Freedom Charter" that called for an end to discrimination and injustice. The charter also demanded the vote for all men and women and an equal share in the country's wealth.

In 1956, the government arrested 156 Congress members. These leaders all went on trial for treason. The trial lasted four years. At that time, the members were found not guilty and set free.

Nelson Mandela, leader of the African National Congress (ANC). In 1962, he began serving a life sentence in prison. He was released from prison early in 1990, and has been traveling all over the world speaking about the terrible situation in his country.

Massacre at Sharpeville

On March 21, 1960, five thousand protesters met outside a police station in the township of Sharpeville. They wanted to protest the Pass Laws. Women and children were in this crowd.

The police opened fire on the frightened protesters without warning. The crowd ran in panic, but the police kept shooting. Sixty-nine people died that day, and 180 were wounded. It would not be the only time policemen shot at unarmed protesters without warning.

The Sharpeville Massacre shocked the world. But nothing could stop the government. Officials just made living conditions worse for blacks. The South African government broke up all anti-apartheid groups. People went to prison without a trial. Many were even tortured.

Antiapartheid people felt very angry. They had tried to be peaceful. The ANC had been peaceful for fifty years. But now certain members decided to try other methods. The ANC set up a special military group called Umkhonto we Sizwe, or "Spear of the Nation." Nelson Mandela became the leader of this group.

Members of Umkhonto we Sizwe did not attack people. Instead, they attacked government property. Another group, called Poqo, began similar actions. Poqo was more violent than the Umkhonto.

By 1965, both groups had been destroyed. The police captured all the leaders and put them on trial. Nelson Mandela received a life sentence, even though he had never killed anyone. He remained in jail for twenty-eight years. He was finally released in February 1990.

Tutu goes to London

All this time, Desmond Tutu worked for his church in South Africa. He showed no signs of being a political protester. He had studied theology for three years and had become a priest.

In 1962, Tutu left South Africa to go to London. He would study theology at King's College and work as an assistant priest. He was thirty-one years old.

Desmond Tutu loved England. He and Leah had trouble with cold weather at first. But London seemed like paradise compared to the troubles of South Africa. No one asked to see passbooks. Desmond and Leah could walk anywhere they wanted and not be arrested.

One day Tutu waited in line at a London bank. A white man pushed in front of him. The bank teller told the man that he would have to wait his turn. This kind of respect would never have happened in South Africa.

British people also had the freedom to say whatever they thought. Tutu discovered Speakers' Corner in Hyde Park. Anyone who had something to say could come here and express his or her opinion. There were even policemen on duty to protect these speakers. Something like this could never have happened under South Africa's racist system.

Desmond Tutu did very well at King's College. He received two degrees in theology there. He also learned Hebrew. Now he knew eight languages — Xhosa, Tswana, Venda, Zulu, English, Afrikaans, Greek, and Hebrew.

The British people loved Tutu. His powerful preaching, his laughter, and his

"[Desmond] told us how the police can knock at the door and take away the husband or the wife, and if a neighbor doesn't happen to see, that person has just gone. . . . they just disappear."

John Ewington, a friend of Desmond Tutu's, in Shirley du Boulay's book Tutu: Voice of the Voiceless

kindness helped relax people. They liked to see him ride around the parish on his motorcycle.

There were many tears when Desmond and his family finally left England. Their British friends gave a farewell party in their honor. Tutu had learned a great deal about religion and politics. He also learned about giving and receiving kindness. He realized again that black and white people could live together in peace, if they wanted to. But now it was time to go home to South Africa.

Police state

When they returned, apartheid was worse than ever. In 1958, Dr. Hendrik Verwoerd had become South Africa's prime minister.

Up until that time, some areas of life had been free from apartheid. Blacks and whites had still lived together in a few areas of the country. Black and white athletes sometimes played professional sports together.

Verwoerd wanted to change that. He hated all black people and believed that the white race would be ruined somehow by coming into contact with other groups. He believed that the white race was in danger and needed protection in order to survive. But the blacks were the people who really needed protection — from apartheid and from Dr. Verwoerd.

"You are told by those who are powerful . . . that you must move from your property because they want it. . . . Your community is being destroyed. You are being asked to abandon your South African citizenship. . . . It is almost as if you are being stoned to death as a community."
Desmond Tutu,
to a group of black villagers

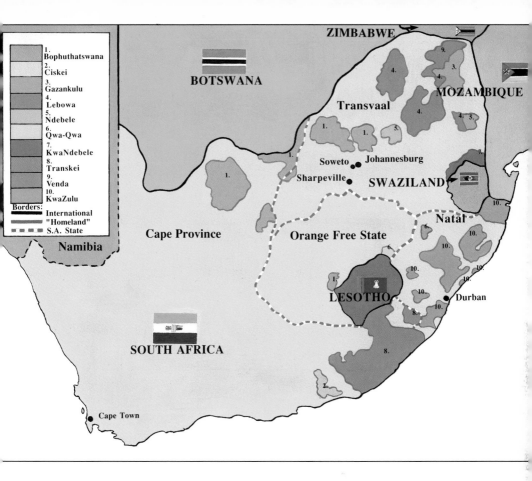

Borders:
International
"Homeland"
S.A. State

1. Bophuthatswana
2. Ciskei
3. Gazankulu
4. Lebowa
5. Ndebele
6. Qwa-Qwa
7. KwaNdebele
8. Transkei
9. Venda
10. KwaZulu

ZIMBABWE

BOTSWANA

MOZAMBIQUE

Transvaal

Soweto — Johannesburg
Sharpeville — SWAZILAND

Cape Province

Orange Free State

Natal

Namibia

LESOTHO — Durban

SOUTH AFRICA

Cape Town

British prime minister Harold Macmillan made a famous speech in 1960. He said South Africa needed to change its government. But no one from the outside offered any real help. Decent South Africans had to try to fight apartheid on their own.

After the Sharpeville Massacre in 1960, there were more new apartheid laws. Black lives were now completely separate from whites'. Black people could not use white buses, beaches, toilets, or sports

The "homelands" are in fact a group of twenty-eight separate pieces of land that were left for the Africans after the whites had moved to occupy the best areas. The "homelands" are among the most crowded areas in Africa. There is very little work available in these unhappy, run-down places.

27

fields. They had to have permission to leave their assigned areas. Any violation meant arrest and prison.

Verwoerd said that each race was different and should "develop separately." He offered blacks separate lands, called Bantustans or "homelands." Most blacks had never seen these "homelands." This was just another way to force black people out of the areas that the whites wanted. These "homelands" were the poorest areas of the country.

Whites took all the best land for themselves. The other racial groups made up 80 percent of the country's population, but they received only 13 percent of the land. The government used the law to

Above: A mother struggles to do her household chores under miserable conditions in Zwelitemba Township When families are forced to leave, they are often left to survive on distant land that whites do not want.

Opposite: This family from Sophiatown was among those forced to move to the so-called homelands, far from their real homes. Their home was then destroyed. Three-and-a-half-million blacks have been treated this way in South Africa since the 1960s.

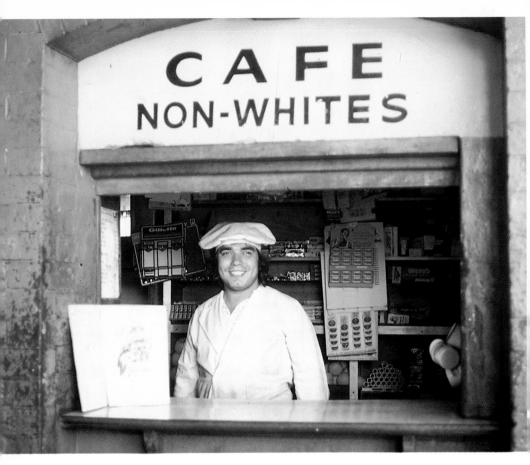

South African blacks, Tutu included, are not allowed to eat in "white" areas. They are served through hatches, like this one, at the side or back of the building.

force blacks out of their homes. Blacks were no longer citizens of South Africa. They had no rights. Black families who had lived in the same place for generations had to leave under the Group Areas Act.

Sophiatown

Sophiatown was a black community of nearly sixty thousand people in Johannesburg, the second largest city in South Africa. Father Trevor Huddleston was the area's parish priest. He tried to save Sophiatown from being destroyed.

The people didn't have a chance to succeed. Two thousand policemen came with eighty trucks. They forced the blacks to leave and destroyed their homes. The government built a new white suburb where Sophiatown once stood. The white leaders named it "Triumph."

Broken families

Most blacks have lived in the poor, dusty "homelands" since the 1960s. The only other choices are "townships," slum areas built outside rich white cities. They are near the cities so that the black people can work for the whites doing jobs that the whites don't want to do.

Apartheid has hurt millions of innocent people. Poverty is everywhere among the blacks. It is almost impossible for blacks to live a decent life. Many families have been torn apart. Poor black fathers

"'Does your mother receive a pension or grant or something?'

'No,' she replied.

'Then what do you do for food?'

'We borrow food,' she answered.

'Have you ever returned any of the food you have borrowed?'

'No.'

'What do you do when you can't borrow food?'

'We drink water to fill our stomachs.'"

Desmond Tutu, talking with a black child from the Zweleding resettlement camp, quoted in Shirley du Boulay's Tutu: Voice of the Voiceless

The Tutu family in London, where Desmond studied for his theology degree. Desmond and Leah are with their four children — left to right: Trevor, Theresa, Naomi, and Mpho.

went to the cities to work. There were no jobs in the Bantustans. Mothers could find jobs only as nannies or domestic servants to white families. People without jobs had to stay out of the cities. So the disabled, the elderly, and the children had to stay behind in the Bantustans.

Desmond Tutu worked for the church during these sad years. He had three degrees when he returned from England. He got a job teaching Greek and theology at the Federal Theological Seminary in the Cape Province.

Tutu led a very religious life. He prayed for long hours every day. He felt a great love for the church.

Tutu saw his country's troubles. The injustice of South Africa's laws hurt him deeply. He knew that no matter how smart he was, there would be no place for him in the apartheid system.

He had no rights simply because he was black. He could not eat in a white café. He could not send his children to a good school. He could not live in a good home. He could not even vote. But Tutu always believed that his religion was more important than anything else.

Turning point

Tutu was a priest at Fort Hare University while teaching at the seminary. Fort Hare was one of only three universities for black students.

Student protests had taken place in the United States and Europe. The students at Fort Hare decided to stage their own protest in 1968. They would ask for some small changes at the university. About five hundred students gathered for a peaceful sit-in on the lawns.

School officials told the students to stop the protest or be expelled. The students sat quietly, reading and talking. The police arrived and attacked the students with armored cars, dogs, and tear gas. At gunpoint, the students packed their belongings and left. This was a terrible punishment for the black students. It took many years just to get permission to go to a university. These young people would probably never get another chance.

This unjust action made Tutu angry. He had never been active in politics before. But now he stood up for the black students and their rights.

Dean of Johannesburg

Tutu continued to teach for the next few years. He was also highly respected in South Africa's Anglican church.

In 1972, Tutu again left South Africa for London. He worked for three years as the associate director of the Theological Education Fund. He visited many countries during this time. He learned a lot about the troubles in the world. This would help him in the years ahead.

Apartheid deprives blacks of rights that other people take for granted, such as the right to live and work where they want. This couple was fired for arguing with another worker. Having been fired, they and their family immediately became homeless. If they can't find work, they must go to a "homeland," where the land is poor.

Soweto, June 16, 1976: Children sing and dance in peaceful protest of a new law that says their lessons must be taught in Afrikaans rather than their native language.

People respected Tutu's kindness, wisdom, and courage. He began to speak out about all of the injustices that he saw around him.

Tutu was elected dean of Johannesburg in 1975. No black had ever held such a high position in the Anglican church before. Black people were excited about Tutu's election. They were very proud of him. Tutu showed his support for fellow blacks by refusing to move to a white suburb. Deans had always lived in a plush home in a white area. But Desmond and his family decided to live in the township of Soweto, twelve miles (19 km) away from his cathedral. This township

"English newspapers . . . would describe an accident in these words: 'Three persons and a Native were injured.'"
    Desmond Tutu,
    in Hope and Suffering

The same demonstration, less than an hour later. The police have opened fire and twelve-year-old Hector Peterson is dead. He is the first of nearly six hundred children to be killed in what became a protest that shook South Africa for months.

is a large area outside of Johannesburg where many poor blacks live.

Letter to the prime minister

Desmond Tutu took a brave political step. He wrote a very polite and respectful letter to the new prime minister, John Vorster. In the letter, Tutu asked for justice and an end to racial discrimination in South Africa. "I write to you, Sir, because, like you, I am deeply committed to real reconciliation with justice for all, and to

"My vision is of a South Africa that is totally non-racial. It will be a society that is more just. . . . Freedom is indivisible. Whites can't enjoy their separate freedoms. They spend too much time and resources defending those freedoms instead of enjoying them."

Desmond Tutu,
in Hope and Suffering

After 1976, young blacks began to lead the struggle against apartheid. They were determined not to give in as their parents had. This young woman is proud to be black.

peaceful change to a more just and open South African society."

Tutu was afraid that a violent struggle for freedom would cause the death of many people. He wrote: "I have a growing nightmarish fear that unless something drastic is done very soon then bloodshed and violence are going to happen in South Africa almost inevitably."

He also warned the prime minister that black people could take only so much injustice. They would soon be desperate and would fight back against the

Opposite: Blacks rioted against apartheid for months after the killings at Soweto. White policemen patrolled the townships in armored cars, trying to put down the uprising (top), while young blacks continued to show their anger on the streets (bottom).

37

Inches away, but worlds apart. White schoolboys leaving a cadet camp in Vereeniging pass a group of young blacks their own age. Because of the apartheid laws, these white boys are not allowed to see how blacks live in their own land. Unfortunately, the only way black boys will see inside white homes is if they are servants.

government. Nothing would be able to stop the violence once it finally began.

Tutu asked Vorster to end the Pass Laws and let black people live in the cities. He urged the prime minister to meet and talk with black leaders. Vorster ignored Tutu's letter. He said Tutu was just trying to cause trouble.

The children of Soweto

Young black people had a new political group called "Black Consciousness." Blacks learned to be proud of their culture and their heritage. These young people understood their country's problems.

The government made a big mistake just one month after Tutu sent his letter.

Officials ordered black schools to stop teaching in English. From now on, the law stated, teachers now had to speak in the language of the whites, Afrikaans.

At first, student protests were quiet and peaceful. The government ignored them. On June 16, 1976, black children marched through the dusty streets of Soweto. This singing, laughing crowd of ten to fifteen thousand schoolchildren walked to a nearby sports stadium, never imagining what was waiting for them.

The police met them with violence. They opened fire on the children. The first victim was twelve-year-old Hector Peterson. Soon there was a national black uprising against apartheid. Children led the riots. Nothing like this had ever happened before. The riots ended after several months. Hundreds of people died. The apartheid government still had the power. But the system had suffered a strong, open challenge.

The police violence in South Africa shocked the world. People all over the world watched their television screens in horror as unarmed, singing students were shot and killed before their eyes. No one could believe this cruelty.

Desmond Tutu was not in South Africa during this sad time. He had been appointed bishop of Lesotho. Tutu devoted his energy to the church. But he felt great pain for his people.

Apartheid, says Tutu, "contradicts the Bible and Christian teaching. That is why it is totally evil and totally immoral." Tutu is a passionate preacher, respected for his knowledge of theology.

Then, on September 12, 1977, South African police murdered Steven Biko. Biko was the founder and leader of Black Consciousness. He had been a fine and gifted man. He had been ready to become the greatest South African leader since Nelson Mandela. Biko was only thirty years old when the police beat and tortured him to death.

Tutu gave an emotional speech at Biko's funeral. His words told how people felt. "We are numb with grief, and groan with anguish 'Oh God, where are you? Oh God, do you really care — how can you let this happen to us?'"

Prayer for white people, too

Tutu believed that apartheid harmed white people, too. It made them lose their concern for others. They forgot their humanity. He asked the people at Biko's funeral to pray for the whites of South Africa. He said that the rulers and the police who had murdered Biko needed special prayers.

Most people did not want to pray for South African whites. Steven Biko had died in terrible pain. But Tutu tried to make them realize that whites were victims, too.

Many whites in South Africa did not see how blacks had to live. White children who were raised in beautiful houses could not imagine what life was like for black children. They couldn't see how black people lived because white people were not allowed in the townships or "homelands." White South Africans were trained to think that separating people by skin color was the right thing to do.

Radio and television stations in South Africa hid the truth from the people. The government controlled, or censored, everything. The people saw only what the government wanted them to see. In fact, people in other countries knew more about injustice in South Africa than did the people who lived there.

The South African government spent a lot of money hiding the truth from the

"If apartheid is dead, then urgent funeral arrangements need to be made. The body is still around and it is making a terrible smell."
Percy Qoboza, editor,
the Post *(Johannesburg)*

people. Television showed how other countries had violence and riots. But South African riots never appeared on the news. People had no real idea of the problems in their country.

The way Desmond Tutu was shown on television in his own country proves how the news was controlled. In person, Tutu's laughter and kindness were clear to everyone. But South African television cut, or "edited," tapes of his speeches. They showed only bits and pieces of his talks. They let the people hear only what might make them angry. They tried to make people dislike Tutu. The government saw him as a troublemaker.

This was very unfair. Tutu has always believed in love and peace. He wanted all his people to be united. He knew that apartheid is an evil system. He said that God created all people equal. Any laws that let one group hurt another are crimes against God. In this way, religion and politics often come together.

Into the hot seat

In 1978, Desmond Tutu received another important position. He returned to South Africa from Lesotho. This time he would stay no matter what happened.

This new job lasted six years. The South African Council of Churches named him its first black general secretary. He was still a bishop, but he did not have a

Opposite: A vision of the future? This type of class, with different racial groups in it, is becoming common in South Africa. It shows how the country might be after apartheid is eliminated. It also shows that Desmond Tutu's vision of racial peace and harmony can work.

parish. He held one of the highest positions in the South African Anglican church. By this time, churches had begun to speak out against apartheid.

The South African government knew that it had to make some changes. The economy was growing very quickly. Businesses needed all the good people they could get. Many people tried to ignore apartheid. They tried to work around the government's strict laws.

The government did end a few apartheid laws. Blacks could use public toilets and go to public parks again. Black and white athletes played sports together. Blacks could now go to a few hotels.

Some government leaders seemed to be concerned about how blacks lived. There was a new prime minister, P. W. Botha. Botha warned whites that apartheid needed changes. "Adapt or die," he told white South Africans.

But the leaders did not really want to change the laws of apartheid. They just wanted to look good to the rest of the world. They promised to make some reforms. Politicians tried to tell the world that apartheid was near its end. But the cruel Pass Laws and Group Areas Act still denied freedom to blacks. Many black families still had to leave their homes. They still had no basic rights.

Small changes did not satisfy younger black people. They were ready for a big

Desmond Tutu addresses a crowd at the funeral of fourteen victims of violence in the black township of Kwathema in 1985. In the late 1970s and early 1980s, he became one of the strongest voices against apartheid. He always speaks against violence and for harmony between blacks and whites.

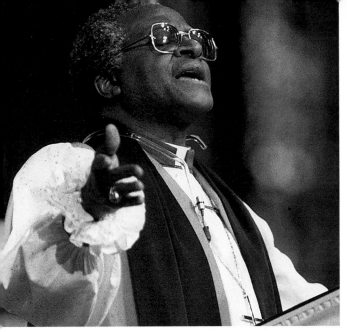

*Four faces of
Desmond Tutu.
Top left: At prayer
during a visit to the
United States in 1984.
Bottom left: Giving an
interview to journalists.
Above (both pictures):
At home in
Johannesburg in 1985.*

45

Christmas, 1987 — Archbishop Tutu enjoys his own Christmas party. He has turned his home in Cape Town into a community center, where black and white children play together. Photographer Omar Badsha, who took this picture, was imprisoned without trial in 1988.

change. They would never accept apartheid the way their parents had. This made whites uneasy. Leaders of the government knew they would need to use more violence to control the blacks. Blacks knew they would have to fight back if they hoped to win any freedom.

Tutu's rising voice

Desmond Tutu was getting stronger in the fight against apartheid. The whole world came to know him as a voice of South African protest.

He had always been a religious person first. But he could also fight for the rights of his people. He traveled to many places asking that apartheid end. He said: "God . . . takes sides. He is not a neutral God. He took the side of the slaves, the oppressed, the victims." Tutu never preached violence. He always asked for peace and unity.

Many white people wished that Tutu would keep politics and religion separate. They didn't like to hear this black bishop blame them for South Africa's problems or demand that they change all of the unfair policies.

Government leaders and news people tried to tell the public that Tutu was a dangerous man. Many of these personal attacks were silly. One newspaper even called him "an insect in dark glasses." Tutu received many threats on the phone. He always listened to what the caller had to say. Then he said a prayer for the caller before hanging up.

Many people really thought Tutu was wrong. They even said he was the devil! Desmond tried not to think too much about these cruel insults and threats. But they still upset him very much. He was upset that people could be so cruel.

Sanctions call

Tutu had many disagreements with his government. These disagreements began to cause serious trouble for him. Officials took his passport away in 1980. Tutu had

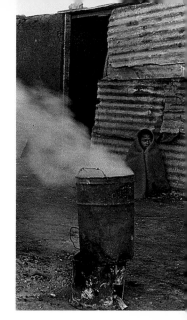

A black child huddles outside a "resettlement shack" (top) while police, carrying whips known as sjamboks, *supervise the area (above).*

47

asked Denmark to stop buying South African coal to protest apartheid. This type of action or penalty is called a "sanction." Bishops from all over the world defended Desmond Tutu. The government had to return his passport.

Also during 1980, the police arrested Tutu during a protest march. They treated him like a criminal. They took his picture and his fingerprints. He had to pay a fine.

In 1981, Tutu visited America. He spoke out against apartheid. Later, he went to Rome and discussed South Africa's problems with Pope John Paul II.

Tutu begged the world to stop trading with South Africa. He especially wanted the support of Britain, the United States, and West Germany. He said that economic sanctions were the last peaceful means of protest available. He asked the South African government to give up apartheid "before it is too late."

Many people thought that sanctions might harm blacks more than help them. But Desmond Tutu was sure of himself. His calls for sanctions caused more anger in South Africa than anything else he ever did. Some people called him a traitor. But Tutu knew there was no other nonviolent way to protest. Most black leaders were in jail. In one way, all this attention was good. Government leaders spoke against Desmond Tutu because they were afraid of his power.

"They chased her across the veld, they beat her. . . . Her mother was crying uncontrollably. The two black clergymen with me couldn't take any more and one . . . said 'Let us pray.' And so we stood there with heads bowed, around a plain kitchen table. . . . And her mother wept on and there were tears in all our eyes: tears for Maki, tears for the beloved country."
David Beresford, reporter for the Guardian (London)

Nobel Peace Prize winner

Desmond Tutu won the Nobel Peace Prize in 1984. This award showed support for Desmond's beliefs. It also showed support for all of the people who fought the apartheid system.

The news of Desmond Tutu's award excited South Africa's black people and others trying to end apartheid. They celebrated and sang for hours. "Hey, we are winning!" Tutu shouted when he heard the good news.

People from all over the world sent their congratulations. Leaders from the United States, Britain, Poland, and India were just a few who called Tutu or sent him telegrams. But the South African government said nothing to Tutu. They would not recognize or show support for this award.

There was more good news. Desmond Tutu had been elected to the position of bishop of Johannesburg.

Bomb scare

Tutu went to Oslo, Norway, to receive the Nobel Prize. Thousands of students gathered to cheer Tutu. They celebrated for four days.

But during the award ceremony there was a bomb scare. Police had to search the building. The people stood outside, singing "We Shall Overcome." After one hour, the police said the building was

These schoolchildren were among three thousand who marched on government offices to protest after black homes in Tsakane were destroyed by government officials in 1985.

Members of the United Democratic Front (UDF) mourn their dead. Mass funerals like this one have become a common place for political protests.

safe. A choir from South Africa sang the black anthem "Nkosi Sikele' iAfrika." Tutu finally received the Nobel Prize.

In his acceptance speech, Tutu called for justice in South Africa. He said: "Let us beat our swords into plowshares."

Bishop Desmond Tutu was now a major figure in world affairs. Millions of people who did not know about apartheid now heard Tutu speak about the system.

Black anger explodes

In 1984, the black people of South Africa exploded with anger. Prime Minister Botha had decided to make a small change. "Coloureds" and Indians could now vote, but only for their own separate government. This was not a good offer. Whites would still keep the real power.

The blacks were insulted by this unfair plan. They had been totally ignored. The

Above, both: Violence occurs as the police and army fail to break the spirit of protesters. In 1988, the most brutal and repressive laws South Africa had ever seen were created to prevent protest. Even reporting violence could mean imprisonment without trial.

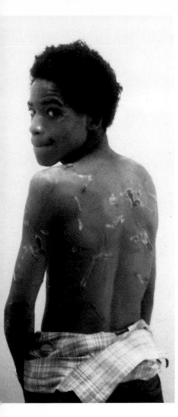

Thirty thousand people were arrested, many without charges, including thousands of children. Some were tortured. Others are still being held. The police have refused to tell families where their children are.

government claimed that blacks were not even citizens of South Africa, but were citizens of the Bantustans, the so-called independent black homelands.

This was a terrible idea. Most blacks had never even seen the "homelands" they were supposed to belong to. No other country in the world accepted these lands as real countries.

Black people could not control their anger any longer. There were many more protests everywhere. As before, the police and army used violence to try to control the people.

Police fought with shotguns, tear gas, and whips called *sjamboks*. Everyone was scared. No one was safe. Thousands of people went to jail without a trial.

Young blacks who called themselves "comrades" caused a new kind of trouble. They accused older blacks of giving in to the government and not trying to fight apartheid. They sometimes took their anger out on other black South Africans.

These "comrades" had a cruel new method of killing. They put what they called "necklaces" around the heads of their victims. These were tires filled with gasoline and set on fire.

Tutu was shocked. It seemed that his dream of peace would never happen. "Why don't we use methods of which we will be proud when our liberation is attained?" He did not want this violence.

"I will pack my bags"

In 1985 Tutu went to a funeral in the Transvaal. The police had killed four black men. The township of Duduza there was like a war zone. Police had killed ten blacks in one week and set their homes on fire. The homes of local leaders and black policemen had also been burned.

Desmond Tutu asked the people to stop the violence. He still wanted to change apartheid peacefully. The crowd did not listen. The people saw a black man they thought was a spy for the police. They ran to kill him, set fire to his car, and shouted "Let the dog die!"

Bishop Tutu holds an all-night vigil to save the people and the small village of Mogopa. Although they had lived there for generations, the next day the whole town was bulldozed and the people were taken away. White farmers bought the villagers' cattle at a quarter of its value.

After becoming the first
black archbishop of
Cape Town, Desmond
moved into the
archbishop's house in
Cape Town (right).
Leah had not wanted to
leave her job in
Johannesburg that
championed the rights
of servants. But she
stood by Desmond as
they entered the most
difficult and dangerous
period of their lives.

54

Desmond begged them to stop. Killing was always wrong. The people would not listen. He had to act right away. So Tutu threw himself into the angry crowd. He dragged the scared and bleeding man to safety.

There was another funeral a few days later in Duduza. The crowd thought that a young mother named Maki Shosona was a spy for the police. A mob beat and burned her to death in front of television cameras. People all over the world saw horrifying pictures of the killing.

At another funeral, Tutu said: "If you do that kind of thing again I will find it difficult to speak for . . . liberation. If the violence continues I will pack my bags, collect my family, and leave this beautiful country that I love."

This made some blacks angry. They were also angry that Tutu agreed to meet with the president of South Africa. Tutu said that talks were needed for peace.

During this time, Botha called for a "state of emergency." This gave the police and army more power than ever.

Archbishop Tutu

In 1986 Desmond Tutu was elected archbishop of Cape Town, the highest position in South Africa's Anglican church. This made Tutu one of the most important people in his country. He was also loved and respected all over the

"The Daily Dispatch used the occasion [of Tutu's being named archbishop] to point out that the apartheid system had been shown to be 'no barrier to his progress.'"
    Shirley du Boulay, in
    Tutu: Voice of the
    Voiceless

"At his age, [one would think Tutu] should hate a little bit more. [But] he believes in the Gospel literally."
    Buti Thiagale, a Roman
    Catholic priest active in the
    Black Consciousness
    movement

world. Now he would lead the South African Anglican church. As archbishop, he would talk on equal terms with world leaders. Yet he could not even vote in his own country because he was black.

The ceremony to install an archbishop is called an "enthronement." This was a wonderful celebration, with singing, dancing, and prayer. Tutu invited many world leaders and famous people to the ceremony. But the South African government tried to ruin the event. The officials refused to allow some of Tutu's guests into the country.

Blacks and whites sat together in Cape Town's St. George's Cathedral that day. Tutu said in a very emotional voice: "How I pray that our Lord would open our eyes so that we would see the real, the true identity of each one of us, that this is not a so-called 'Coloured,' or white, or black or Indian, but a brother, a sister — and treat each other as such."

An archbishop first

Archbishop Tutu's religion was more important than ever. "If I do not spend a reasonable amount of time in meditation early in the morning, then I feel a physical discomfort. It is worse than having forgotten to brush my teeth!"

During the day, Tutu received foreign visitors and gave interviews. He gave advice to his bishops and priests. He took

Top: Violent racists such as Eugene Terre Blanche are gaining power. Above: No matter how much these children and their parents resist change, change is coming.

breaks for prayer, lunch, and a short nap in the afternoon. This routine kept his days busy and organized.

The South African press began to show Desmond Tutu's religious side. Many people had not known how devoted he was to his beliefs. Many South Africans had been against his appointment as archbishop. But fellow bishops knew that Tutu was right for leadership.

Tutu knew he needed to be political as well as religious. New laws stopped all antiapartheid groups. The churches were the only hope left.

South Africa's state of emergency was very cruel. The police and army had terrible power. They could jail, torture, and kill anyone they wanted to. They did not allow television cameras where there was trouble. They controlled the press.

A new, evil group gained power. This group was a hate-filled white party called the Afrikaner Resistance Movement. Its members carried flags that reminded the world of the Nazis. The group wanted stricter laws against the blacks. They said Botha, now president, was too peaceful!

"We shall be free"

Black South Africans have not given up on their fight for freedom. They know apartheid will not last forever. But some experts say apartheid is strong enough to last a long time.

History has shown that people cannot be deprived of freedom for too long. Archbishop Desmond Tutu and millions of other South Africans of many colors believe that the nightmare *must* finally come to an end.

As Tutu has said: "Many more will be detained. Many more will be banned. Many more will be deported and killed. Nothing will stop us from becoming free — no police bullets, dogs, tear gas, prison, death, no, nothing will stop us because God is on our side."

Marriage between blacks and whites is once again allowed by the state. Tutu always stresses that individual people of different races generally get along well together.

To find out more . . .

Organizations

The organizations listed below can provide you with information about South Africa, apartheid, and the black experience world-wide. When you write to them, be sure to tell them exactly what you would like to know and always remember to include your name, address, and age.

Africa News Service
P.O. Box 3851
Durham, NC 27702

African National Congress of South Africa (ANC)
P.O. Box 15575
Washington, DC 20003-9997

American Committee on Africa
198 Broadway, Suite 402
New York, NY 10038

Amnesty International
322 Eighth Avenue
New York, NY 10001

Congress of Racial Equality (CORE)
1457 Flatbush Avenue
Brooklyn, NY 11210

Pan-Africanist Congress of Azania (PAC)
211 East 43rd Street, Suite 506
New York, NY 10017

TransAfrica Forum
545 Eighth Street SE
Washington, DC 20003

United Nations Center Against Apartheid
United Nations
New York, NY 10017

Books

Biko. Donald Woods (Random House)

Every Kid's Guide to Understanding Human Rights. Joy Berry
(Childrens Press)

Nelson and Winnie Mandela. John Vail (Chelsea House)

Nelson Mandela: South Africa's Silent Voice of Protest. J. Hargrove
(Childrens Press)

The Peace Seekers: The Nobel Peace Prize. Nathan Aaseng (Lerner)

South Africa. Mike Evans (Franklin Watts)

South Africa. R. Conrad Stein (Childrens Press)

South Africa in Pictures. Department of Geography, Lerner
Publications (Lerner)

Taking A Stand Against Human Rights Abuse. Michael
Kronenwetter (Franklin Watts)

We Live in South Africa. Preben Kristensen and Fiona Cameron
(Franklin Watts)

Winnie Mandela: The Soul of South Africa. Milton Meltzer (Penguin)

List of new words

African National Congress (ANC)
A group that works for equal rights in South Africa. The ANC
was banned by the country's government in 1960, but became
legal again in 1990.

Afrikaans
The language invented and spoken by the Boers, the first white
settlers in South Africa. The language is a mixture of German,
Dutch, and English.

apartheid
A word that means "apart-hood." Under an apartheid system,
races are kept separate by law. South Africa has such a system.

archbishop

The highest rank of bishop. An archbishop has control of his church and the churches of other bishops in the area. As archbishop of Cape Town, Tutu has all of South Africa as his area.

Bantustans

The so-called independent homelands where all black South Africans had to live. These poor areas could not support the people who lived in them.

"Black Consciousness"

A peaceful antiapartheid movement started by Steven Biko. It taught black people to be proud of their culture and heritage.

Boer War

A war between the Boers and Great Britain that took place from 1899 to 1902. Both sides wanted to control the South African gold fields.

Boers

Descendants of the first Dutch, French, and German settlers of South Africa. They are also called "Afrikaners."

censorship

The act of keeping any unwanted information out of the mail, the press, or television. For example, the South African government censors reports of black protest. The government keeps much of its power through the use of censorship.

"Coloureds"

In South Africa, a "racial" group that is neither totally black nor white. It usually refers to people who have parents of two races.

discriminate

To treat a person or group unfairly because of race, sex, religion, or some other reason.

Group Areas Act
A South African law passed in 1950. Under it, people had to live and work in special areas based on skin color.

kaffir
An insulting word that means "infidel," or nonbeliever. Many whites use this word to insult blacks in South Africa.

massacre
To kill a large number of people. Sixty-nine people were killed by police in the Sharpeville Massacre in South Africa in 1960.

Nazis
Members of the National Socialist German Workers' party. The Nazis were a cruel white racist group that wanted to rule the world during the 1930s and 1940s. They killed millions of innocent people and wanted "racial purity." The Nazis wanted only "racially pure" white people to have freedom.

"Nkosi Sikele' iAfrika"
The beautiful black anthem of South Africa. The title means "God Bless Africa."

Nobel Prizes
Prizes awarded each year to people who have done special work in a certain field. Nobel Prizes are given in medicine, chemistry, physics, literature, economics, and peace. Desmond Tutu won the Nobel Peace Prize in 1984.

Poqo
A word that means "standing alone." It is the name of a South African antiapartheid military group of the 1960s.

protest
To speak out against something that people think should be changed; to gather together to oppose a government or other policy.

racism

The idea that one race is better than others. Apartheid is a way of life based on racism.

riot

A group of people who are acting out of control, often in protest of something. Riots are often very violent.

sanction

A nonviolent way to protest something in which nations refuse to trade with or sell to another country because they disagree with its policies. Many countries now have economic sanctions against South Africa.

theology

The study of God and religion. Desmond Tutu has two degrees in theology.

Umkhonto we Sizwe

In English, "Spear of the Nation." A military group of the African National Congress. Nelson Mandela led this group until the South African government broke it up in 1962.

Voortrekkers

The first Boers to settle the northeastern part of South Africa. They movedthere to escape British control.

Important dates

1652   The Dutch East India Company settles the first whites at Cape Town.

1795   Great Britain takes over the Cape Colony.

1833   British rulers demand that the Boers free their slaves.

1837   Thousands of Afrikaners begin the "Great Trek" north.

1899-1902	The British fight and win the Boer War. Thousands of Boers die in British concentration camps.
1910	The Union of South Africa is formed out of Boer and British territories. Blacks are not allowed to take part.
1912	The African National Congress (ANC) is formed.
1931	**October 7** — Desmond Mpilo Tutu is born at Klerksdorp, 120 miles (193 km) from Johannesburg.
1936	Blacks' right to vote is abolished.
1947	Tutu is hospitalized with tuberculosis and becomes friends with Father Trevor Huddleston.
1948	The National party wins the general election on an apartheid platform.
1952	The ANC's Defiance Campaign raises its membership from seven thousand to 100 thousand.
1954	Tutu receives his teacher's diploma.
1955	The Bantu Education Act is passed. This law makes it illegal for black schools to teach math and science. **July 2** — Tutu marries Leah Nomalizo Shenxane.
1956-1961	The government arrests 156 ANC members and tries them for treason, but they are eventually acquitted.
1958	Tutu enters St. Peter's Theological College to begin religious training.
1959	Eight Bantustans, or "homelands," are set up by the government. Millions of blacks are forced from their homes to live in these distant areas.

1960   **March 21** — The Pan-Africanist Congress (PAC) gathers five thousand blacks in the Sharpeville township to protest against the Pass Laws. Police open fire into the crowd, killing 69 people and wounding 180.

1961   Nelson Mandela forms Umkhonto we Sizwe, a military division of the ANC.
Tutu is ordained a priest.

1962   Nelson Mandela is arrested and later sentenced to life in prison.
September — Tutu goes to London to study theology at King's College.

1968   Tutu returns to South Africa to teach at St. Peter's College, Alice. While there, black students are attacked by police during a peaceful demonstration. The incident is a turning point for Tutu.

1970   Tutu begins his duties as lecturer at the University of Botswana, Lesotho, and Swaziland.

1972   Tutu becomes associate director of the Theological Education Fund in London.

1975   Tutu becomes dean of Johannesburg.
The government states that arithmetic and social studies may now be taught in black schools. But at the same time, the government orders black schools to stop teaching in English. Teachers are to speak in the Afrikaans language.

1976   Tutu writes to Prime Minister Vorster, warning of the violence that will happen if oppression continues.
June 16 — A peaceful demonstration by black school-children in Soweto is fired on by police.
July — Tutu becomes bishop of Lesotho.

1977 September 12 — Steven Biko dies in police custody. World protest erupts against apartheid. Tutu speaks at the funeral.

1978 Tutu becomes general secretary of the South African Council of Churches.
P. W. Botha becomes prime minister.

1979 Tutu calls for economic sanctions against the South African government on Danish television.

1983 Prime Minister Botha calls for a referendum on a new parliament that will include whites, "Indians," and "Coloureds," but not blacks. Only whites may vote.

1984 December — Tutu receives the Nobel Peace Prize.

1985 February 3 — Tutu is named bishop of Johannesburg.

1986 April — Tutu is elected archbishop of Cape Town, head of the Anglican church in South Africa.
June — P. W. Botha, president under the new constitution, declares a state of emergency to deal with black unrest.

1988 Botha bans all remaining antiapartheid groups. Police are given unlimited powers of arrest.
August — The Trade Union Building in Johannesburg, headquarters of Tutu and antiapartheid groups, is destroyed by a bomb.

1989 September — F. W. de Klerk is elected president. He vows to establish a bill of rights for all races.

1990 February — Nelson Mandela is freed from prison.
June — Mandela visits the United States and speaks out strongly against apartheid.

Index